P9-CMY-275

The Before And

HOUGHTON MIFFLIN COMPANY Boston / New York / London 1992

*For Jackson*

---



ISBN 0-395-63198-X
ISBN 0-395-60905-4 (pbk.)

Color design and hand coloring by
Dizzy Fish Studios, Siesta Key, Florida

Printed in the United States of America

HOR 10 9 8 7 6 5 4 3 2 1

# BEFORE

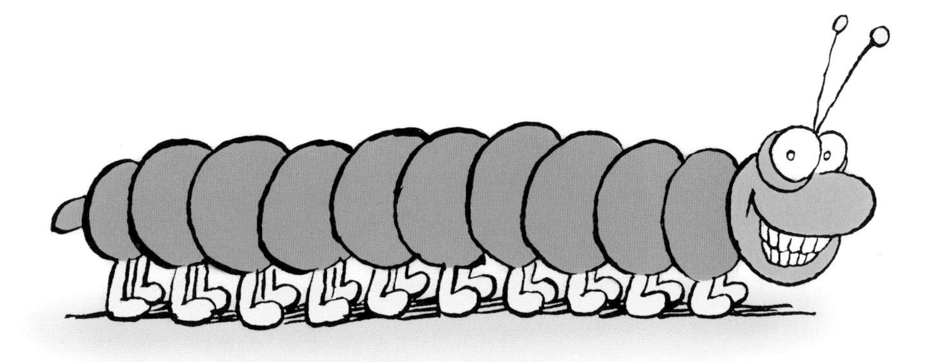

# AFTER

# BEFORE

# AFTER

# Before

# After

# BEFORE

# AFTER

# Before

# After

# BEFORE

# AFTER

# Before

# After

# BEFORE

# AFTER

# Before

# After

# BEFORE

# AFTER

# Before

# After

# BEFORE

# AFTER

# before

# after

before

# after

# Before

# After

# Before

# After

# BEFORE

# AFTER

# BEFORE

# AFTER

# Before

# After

# Before

# After

# BEFORE

# AFTER

# BEFORE

# AFTER